The Flipping Book

A quick guide to the basics of real estate
Investment

By William Lynn

Preface

This book is designed to give you the basic knowledge of how the flipping business works and give you an idea if you want to get involved and have your money involved in it. This book will not make you an expert in the business of flipping properties. Unlike other books this is explained in a simple easy to read short format and it is explained from a realistic perspective. This is not a get rich quick business and this is not a book to exploit your interest in the business. This business is very dangerous and carries many risks of money and property loss. This book is here to arm you with the basics so you can make the educated choice on whether or not to get involved.

In this book there are a lot of generalizations, the reason for this is the laws change from state to state. It is important for you to do the leg work and find out what the laws are and how they protect or hinder your business choices. I can only speak for the states I have worked in and laws I have heard of in other states. If it is an area where I believe the laws to be different than the laws I know, I have tried to make note of that. I also will not give recommendations for companies or services to use. It is up to you to find the best suited companies to help you with your tasks.

I have combined years of experience in real estate, construction, trustee sales and flipping that are well over a decade of expertise. It is vitally important you gain some knowledge in any or all of these and also include some legal experience if possible before venturing into the business of flipping properties. It is more dangerous for your money to be played with in this business, without some strong knowledge, than to give it to a business man you don't know to let them make you money. I do not advise doing that in any way shape or form without knowing who the person is. You will have to take responsibility for your money if you ever plan to make money in this business.

With all that said good luck and I hope this book gives you some insight into the world of flipping properties.

Table of contents

Section 1: Real estate

*Chapter 1: Basics of real estate

*Chapter 2: Buying real estate

*Chapter 3: Types of sales of real estate

Section 2: Buying real estate

*Chapter 4: Lien sales

*Chapter 5: Funding your flip

Section 3: Trustee sales

*Chapter 6: Buying at trustee sales

*Chapter 7: Requirements to buy at trustee sales

*Chapter 8: How to bid

*Chapter 9: Strategies for bidding

*Chapter 10: What happens next/ Where do I get my keys?

Section 4: Occupancy and renting

*Chapter 11: Leaving tenants in place and renting

*Chapter 12: Cash for keys and evictions

*Chapter 13: No occupant

Section 5: Repairing your property

*Chapter 14: Self fixer upper vs. contractor

*Chapter 15: Things always fixed

*Chapter 16: Things sometimes fixed

*Chapter 17: Things never fixed

Section 6: Moving your investment/ Selling

*Chapter 18: Selling your investment property

*Chapter 19: Sorting through the offers

*Chapter 20: Escrow

Section 7: Your next steps and drawbacks

*Chapter 21: Getting into another project

*Chapter 22: Becoming a large company

*Chapter 23: One man operation vs. company machine

*Chapter 24: Downfalls of the business

*Chapter25: The good side of the business

Section 1

Real Estate

Chapter 1

Basics of Real Estate

Chapter 1 Basics of real estate

Real estate is described as multiple things. First and foremost it is immoveable. As opposed to personal property, which is moveable, also known as chattel or chattel real which is anything you can put on real estate not bolted down. Property comes with rights and interests for the person who owns said property. Property is the right of ownership of anything but in the real estate world, it is a term that also describes a piece of real estate. Personal property, chattel, has its own set of laws that cover it and primarily is protected by law enforcement. Real property or real estate is protected by law enforcement but generally carried out by the court system. Your rights with real estate cover your land, anything built on the land, incidentally attached to it also know as appurtenant to the land and your real estate is immovable. Your real estate rights run from the corners of your land straight down to a point in the middle the land at the center of the earth and from the four corners of the land to space. All state and local governments have slight variations on these rights but this is considered the standard norm.

When buying real estate it is important to know what your rights are, each state changes things that could affect your rights. Some states do not cover water rights on your land. The water may belong to the state as part of a water way or municipal drinking water system. Some types of real estate include chattel as part of the purchase normally in commercial property deals. If you bought a restaurant the kitchen equipment typically comes with the building and if a commercial tenant improves the building the improvements are not always required to be removed. Some states will not have the mineral rights run appurtenant because at some point the mineral rights might have been sold or they already belong to the state.

Encumbrances are another important thing to consider when buying real estate. An encumbrance is rights of others to the land other than the current owner.

The most common type of encumbrance is a mortgage but also includes liens, judgments, special assessments (mello roos), easements, zoning restrictions and encroachments. Liens are money owed and are documents to discharge a debt or obligation and include mechanics liens, tax liens, attachments and a mortgage. Judgments do not always stay with the land but it is important to know if the judgment stays with the previous owner or follows the land because they can become your responsibility. Special assessments or mello roos are government bonds used to pay for infrastructure for the use of real estate owners in the area, such as roads, street lights, sidewalks, underground utilities and schools. These are made to be paid for by the owners over a long period of time and will transfer with the real estate and are disclosed upon transfer. Some of the before mentioned encumbrances affect your use of the land. Easements typically are rights for others to cross your land to get to their land or the city to use for any number of reasons but normally for possible future road development. Zoning restrictions will not let you build a shopping mall on residentially zoned land and vise versa. Typically it is better to buy land zoned for the use you require then try to fight city hall to have the use changed to suit your needs. Encroachments are wrongful placement of an improvement by anyone other than the owner and can be naturally occurring such as an overhanging tree. If the encroachment is not acted upon for a required amount of time, the encroachment can become an easement but this is not always the case.

Again it is always best to know state and local laws when purchasing real estate and for the purposes of an investment. It is better to have a working knowledge of the real estate business in the area you intend to buy in. I would suggest acquiring a real estate sales persons or broker's license before considering getting into a real estate investment. The other option would be hiring a real estate agent to help with the transfer of the property with a working knowledge of the type of purchase you require and enough knowledge to answer any questions you have about the transaction.

Chapter 2

Buying Real Estate

Chapter 2   Buying real estate

Buying real estate can be done in a few different ways and each has its advantages. You can buy real estate the traditional way, get an agent, submit an offer (once the offer is accepted), put it in escrow and upon close of escrow receive title (so long as the property is paid for in full). There are also many types of sales other than a traditional sale which I will get into in the next chapter. You can also do it yourself while it is not required you be an agent or broker to buy real estate it is always advised that you do become one of the two, there are many laws that could easily be misunderstood if the time is not taken to have the knowledge of how they work and why. The main advantage of being your own agent is you would not have to pay someone to do your paperwork for you which over multiple deals can be tens of thousands of dollars. The advantage to hiring an agent is of course not having to go to school to learn the required knowledge and having someone to blame if things are not disclosed. If you are just buying one property and just getting into the business it is probably best to hire an agent but still having a basic understanding of real estate will be very helpful to you.

You and your agent can find a property through what is call the multi listing service or for our purpose and a commonly used shortening of the name (MLS). The MLS is controlled by the local governing body of realtors in your area and the (NAR) national association of realtors. It is not required that you become a realtor to use the MLS. It does require you paying a higher amount than the realtors who have the ability to use it. Most of the information is available online and free of charge but is not updated frequently. A hired agent will be a member of your local group and have access to updated listings. They will have access to properties in your area that you can place offers on and an agent may have leads to properties that have not yet been placed on the market, that you could be interested in.

If you become an agent or broker it is good to know the difference. An agent is a sales person for a brokerage house and has the ability to use the MLS, show you properties, submit offers on properties, host open houses and communicate with agents on the other side of the deal. In other words they can get a limited amount of information from the agent representing the seller of the property. It is limited because if they do not know they can not guess it is against the law to misinform you and because there is only so much information the law allows your agent to disclose to you and the agent representing the seller can only disclose so much without infringing on each other's rights. If you are selling the property it works the same way. For example the seller's agent may tell your agent there are offers on the property but they can not tell your agent how many offers or how much the offers are for. Only so much information is legally allowed to be disclosed. Becoming an agent requires schooling that can be done online or in a classroom and a test administered by the state which can lead to acquiring a sales person's license. The schooling generally is a few classes, some book reading and some self taken prep tests or quizzes.

A broker is a person who has the license the next level higher, which gives them all the rights of a sales person's license and the ability to have agents working under them. This relationship is often called a brokerage. While a brokerage may have more than one broker working for them, if the firm is large enough, it is only required for the purpose of having agents work for you. The advantage to being a broker is the agents who work below you are required to share a portion of their commissions for each deal for the ability to have a place to work. If an agent plans to work in the profession of real estate it is required that they work for a broker. Depending on the level of experience of the agent will determine the percentage the agent is willing to give to the broker. A new agent will give a much larger amount up to 100% (some brokerages require this for the first few deals to cover the expenses to train them). A very experienced agent is more likely to receive 90% of their commission, the remainder is normally to cover the cost of their insurance and a little overhead and the brokerage is very unlikely to have trouble with that agent. The disadvantage to being a broker is you and your business, the brokerage, carry all the liability if an agent makes mistakes that lead to lawsuits. Becoming a broker requires all the schooling and information of the sales person's license, added classes and a much longer state administered test.

The requirements to be an agent or a broker had not changed for many years but in the last 20 years with all of the recessions we have had, that caused large down turns in the housing market, it also caused stricter agent laws. The laws have been changing more and more rapidly which have lead to more classes, harder tests and harder requirements to renew licenses. Make sure to check with the department of real estate (DRE) to find out what the most current and up to date requirements are before becoming an agent or broker. Simple things like finger prints have been changed to live scans and can affect your level of interest in becoming an agent or broker. In this business it is important to have this knowledge, do not let the little things shake you from helpful information and a possible career option.

Chapter 3

Types of Sales of Real Estate

Chapter 3   Types of sales of real estate

When buying real estate through a traditional sale there are three main types of properties you will have available to you. A regular property listing, a short sale and an REO or bank owned property (it stands for Real Estate Owned, which doesn't make much sense for, bank owned property but it is the accepted term used). All of these types of sales are available for agents to look up on the MLS and place offers on. Before a property becomes an REO or government owned (from a lien sale) there are a few types of sales offered to the public that are not available through the MLS. Sheriff sales and trustee sales are the most common type which will be talked about in the next chapter.

With a regular listing the person who owns the property has placed a piece of real estate on the market using an agent or by themselves. It is not always the case that they will make money on the property but the most important factor is that the value of the property is higher than the amount owed on the loan. Any remainder on the loan can be made up by the sale of the property and/or cash paid by the owner and is expected if the property is to sell this way. Normally standard or regular sales are on properties where the owner will receive more money than is owed and will result in profits used toward the purchase of their next property, which is called upgrading a property.

An REO or bank owned property is normally a property that the previous owner has walked away from the loan or the property has been foreclosed on. If the property was foreclosed on it was offered at a foreclosure sale (trustee sale), it did not sell at auction and became bank owned. The difference here is your offers are submitted to a bank representative who evaluates all the offers for the bank. Often times REO properties have not been repaired from possible damage caused by use or vandalism and are sometimes offered at a discount. The discount is usually what the bank feels is enough money to repair the property but in a booming market will normally be erased by offers exceeding the discount. Sometimes the bank will take the liberty of repairing the property if they feel they can get more money than they put into it by the increase in offer price. In other words a property worth $200,000 gets $10,000 in repairs and now brings the bank $225,000 in offers. The $10,000 investment in the property brings $15,000 above what was formerly expected. Most often times you don't see this, banks are in the business of lending money not spending money. A slight return is not always noticed by a large institution even when the number is around a 10% increase in offering price.

A short sale is a tricky type of sale, it is a property that is being sold by the owner and the market does not support a price higher than the amount owed on the loan. Often times the bank will require the home owner to be in default on the property before they will even consider a short sale offer. For a home owner to be in default they have to stop paying on their mortgage for long enough for the bank to start the foreclosure process with a default notice. If you are trying to buy a short sale property, you would submit an offer to the home owner, the same as a standard sale. Once the offer is accepted by the home owner the property will not go into escrow until the bank signs off on it also. Many times agents call properties approved short sales which mean the bank will entertain an offer but it does not mean the bank will accept an offer. Sometimes banks get so back logged it can take up to six month for them to look at the offer. This still does not mean they will accept it and often they are rejected or the party putting in the offer will find something else before the bank gets back with an answer. A short sale is basically asking the bank if they will lose money on the property because the owner can not pay for it anymore. This use to be used as an attempt to slow the foreclosure process but recent legislation will not allow what is called a dual track foreclosure. Dual track just means trying to do a short sale and a foreclosure at the same time or two paths to solve the same problem. In the past these dual tracks took even longer because during foreclosure the bank would have to stop and look at the offers on it. Now if the property is an approved short sale it stops the foreclosure process completely until all the offers have been reviewed.

Section 2

Buying Real Estate

Chapter 4
Lien Sales

Chapter 4 Lien sales

The two most common types of foreclosure sales and/or lien sales are trustee sales and Sheriff Sales. These sales represent the highest amount of profit and largest amount of risk for any investor looking to acquire property. Properties at these types of sales can be bought for up to 50% off but in a more likely situation 20% off of the current market value. These properties can require large amounts of money to repair to make marketable. These properties can also be turnkey, ready to sell, but with the right amount of information they can be very profitable investments.

A trustee sale is a sale conducted by the trust company that holds the title of a property. It is a required part of the foreclosure process and does not guarantee that the property will be sold at a realistic price for the market at that time. When a person takes out a mortgage, in most states, it is required that a bank appoints a trust to hold the title of the property to avoid any miss doing by the bank. In many cases the banks actually owns the trust companies they use to hold the title, solidifying their position on a mortgage and giving them all the control. A smaller lender will have to hire a trust company to hold the title and conduct the sale of the property. A trustee sale does not guarantee that the mortgage you are purchasing is in the first mortgage position giving you the right of ownership on the property. Also a trustee sale is conducted like an auction and is sold to the highest bidder. These are very dangerous sales and you do not have the ability to walk through the property before the time of the sale. If you have not done your homework on a trustee sale you can lose a lot of money very quickly. The advantage to a trustee sale is the potential to buy the property at a large discount and these sales draw everyone from a one time buyer to large hedge funds represented by large companies holding potentially billions of dollars to use at trustee sales nationwide. There is a lot to know about trustee sale and we will revisit this topic later.

The last type of sale is a sheriff sale, it is very similar to a trustee sale and it is conducted like an auction. In states where a trust is not required a court does the preceding of the foreclosure. This type of sale is also used for government tax lien sales, when a home owner owes back taxes on their property and the government is foreclosing on the property for the money owed. These sales are conducted in a courtroom and the sale is conducted by a court appointed sheriff, which is where it gets its name. Sheriff sales also have the advantage of discount on the property but have the disadvantage of a two year right of redemption. Which means at any point within two year of the sale the previous owner may pay back what was owed on the property and take back ownership of the property. Basically making the property useless to the new owner for two years unless you are willing to sue the previous owner for anything you have invested in the property during that time. Which, in most instances, can not be recovered because if they didn't have the money to pay what was owed, what is to say they now have the money to pay you for the money lost to improve or repair the property.

Chapter 5

Funding Your Flip

Chapter 5   Funding your flip

You want to buy a piece of real estate but you don't have the money to buy it right now. This is one of the most common reasons for not getting into the game. There are a great number of ways to get a project funded, smaller projects require less capital and ultimately less overall risk. This is not to say that using someone else's money to fund a project does not carry a large amount of risk, your financial risk overall becomes much greater by using different types of loans and larger amounts of money. Some of the more common types are business loans/lines of credit, second loans on primary properties, hard money loans and investors.

If you own a business already and normally if that business is already in real estate you can get a line of credit from the bank you use already. You need to draw up a business plan and a have a detailed explanation of what you are doing with this property and how you intend to make money on it. This will give the bank the incentive to give you the money, you should also be in good standing with the bank and have a high credit score to get the best rates on the money you are barrowing. You can always shop around the rate you are offered with other financial institutions to find a better rate. If you do not have a business and want to set one up to go ask for money, be aware banks are smart enough to not give money like that. A bank will want to see two years of tax records supporting that you can borrow a large amount of money and your business plan will work as an expansion of your business. The best you will do without it is the bank may feel generous enough to offer your new business a small loan of $50,000 at the rates and terms of a personal loan. This will require the owner of the business to have the best credit possible and a standing good relationship with that bank.

Taking a second on your primary residence is another option. The money will have to be paid back over a long term like a primary mortgage but will cost a significantly larger amount of money. Second loans are approximately double what the going primary mortgage rate is, this is not a specific number but more of a rule of thumb. If the going rate is 8% for a primary or first loan with your level of credit you can expect to see numbers around 16% for your second. Banks will factor in the higher interest against the principal you intend to take from your property and will not let you exceed current market value of your primary residence. Let's say you owe $100,000 on a property currently worth $300,000 the most you could barrow would be $200,000, less whatever the interest rate will be for your loan over your loan term and they will remove a portion of the $200,000 so you still have equity in the property. Equity is the money you have invested in the property and in a booming market your property will grow in equity without you adding extra to the amount invested. Each bank will figure the number a little differently but you are not going to get all of your equity in the loan. Second mortgages carry higher risk then a business loan for the simple reason that if you can't pay back your second mortgage you could lose your primary residence as well as your investment property. You should carefully consider your options before risking your residence to make more money and if you do risk it make sure to save enough money for a few extra payments in case your property takes too long to sell or rent out.

A hard money loan tends to be the closest thing to loan sharking legally allowed by law. If the current rate of a business loan/line of credit is 10% the hard money loan will roughly cost you 18% plus 2 points. A point is a cute way for lenders to charge you interest without calling it interest. 1 point normally works out to be 2% and they generally have to be paid up front. We are basically talking about a 22% interest loan. The advantage is these loans are fairly easy to get and they normally only lend the money for a short term of 6 months to 1 year. These loans are made for people who flip and need the money as soon as possible. The properties you buy are the equity you use against the money you are barrowing and defaulting would cause a forfeiture of the properties in most cases. Where people get into trouble with hard money is when they over estimate the value and under estimate the repair cost of the property, also when a property sits on a stale market for too long and loses value from lack of interest. After you buy it, you do all the work to fix it and then sell it but you still end up owing the hard money lender when you have over valued the property. These types of loans do not work for a buyer who plans to rent the property because the term is too short and the money will be called back before you can even rent it out. These loans are very risky and do have their purpose in the business but if you can get money elsewhere I would recommend doing that.

The last way, I am going to go into, of getting money is investors. Investors are the most common way to fund a project of this size requiring this kind of capital. Acquiring investors is much easier then it would seem. People with lots of money are always looking for ways to make their money into more money with doing as little as possible to gain it. You would have to write up a proposal of what you intend to do and how you intend to do it with a detailed explanation of what the investor will be getting for their money. The best way to explain to your potential investor how low risk it is for them is to back their money with the properties you buy and make sure they understand they can not take their money out until a property has been sold. Most investors will want to see some level of experience in the field you buying into. If you have never done this before and have no experience in real estate you will come off to an investor like a person with the plaque. The most common type of person who has an investment group that flips properties or rents them out for profit are real estate agents who have been in the business for a respectable amount of time. The advantage to investors is you quickly gain the capital you need to flip properties. The disadvantage is you make less money for all the work you did on the project. Your investors will take whatever agreed upon percentage of each property and investors are needy. Investors want updates, progress reports and phone calls answered whenever they call. It is always good to set down right away that your investors are to be silent investors and that they are not partners. Partners have the right to make decisions and change the way things are done, which may conflict with how you want to do them.

Section 3

Trustee Sales

Chapter 6

Buying at Trustee Sales

Chapter 6   Buying at trustee sales

For our purposes we are going to talk heavily about bidding at trustee sales. Since trustee sales bring the most possible profit and always seems attractive to flippers and investors. These sales also bring the highest amount of risk because it takes some serious strategy and preparation to become good at it, while still trying to make money. If you did not do your homework on each possible investment property you could easily lose everything you have with little effort.

Homework as people in the trustee sale business call it, is all the back office information you need to buy something and making an educated guess on what you are buying. Your homework will include, getting up to the minute information on what is happening with the sale of the property, checking title, checking realistic comparison properties in the area(also known as comps), sending a driver to run to the property and last bidding on the property. If you have not done all of these things you could lose your money and you will get the reputation of being a jumper. A jumper is a trade name for a person who doesn't do their homework and tries to guess if they should bid based on the consistency of other buyers in their bidding area. This is dangerous and typically jumpers end up losing a lot of money on one deal because they jumped someone who set them up for failure or becoming too cocky about who they bid against. In other words they normally drive themselves out of business.

Getting up to the minute information about the sale of a property is easy and a lot of people like to try and make it hard. The county that you are buying in offers, normally for free, information on everything set to sell that day. They do not update this information quickly so it is not a fast way to find the information you are looking for. It is a free way to find what is set to sell for each day but the information of whether or not it will sell, postpone to another day or how much the opening price will be, will not be there. Each trustee who is selling properties at your sales site will offer a phone number, website or both, normally free of charge but not always, to possible bidders who come to the sales. The auctioneer will most likely have this information for you. This is still not the best way because it only covers one trustee's group of sales and following multiple sales with multiple auctioneers at multiple times can become difficult. Since I will not promote one company over the other, I will say that the best way to have information available quickly is to pay a compiling company which can be found online. There are quite a few out there, some are more popular than others, but for a small fee, normally per month, these sites will offer you the ability to follow all of the sales in that county for the day, including times of the sale (which is important), trustee sales number and which trustee is selling the property. The time of the sale and trustee, which will give you enough information to know which auctioneer is offering the property you are interested in. The trustee sales number (TS number) will allow the auctioneer to be able to find the property in the list of things set for the day. Most people believe the address is important but any auctioneer with more than a handful of properties will not know or be able to find it quickly by address.

Checking the title on a property is very important, without doing so you could be liable for tens of thousands of dollars in back taxes, fines and judgments against a property. You should also check the court records on the previous owner if you see that the owner has a bankruptcy in process. This will let you know if the property has been released to sell by the bankruptcy courts. Checking the title is easy enough, you need to hire a title representative (title rep) they can check all the information on the property for you and will normally help you sort through it all. Each title company charges a different amount for the service so it is best to shop around and also to use one you have a good relationship with. The only other way to check title is tedious and requires looking through the counties documentation on the property. This would take more time then you may have to get ready for the sale. The main reason for a title search is to check the chain of title to see if the current owner owes any back taxes. If the city has levied any fines against the property for things like poor yard up keep, dead cars in the street or mosquito larva in a pool. It is also to check if mechanics liens have been put on the property. Mechanics liens are caused by contractors who worked on the property and have not been paid by the previous owner.

Checking comps is probably the easiest of all the tasks to do when doing your homework. You go online to any good real estate web site and check all the properties of similar floor plans and similar square footage properties with similar features, within a few miles of your target property. Do not use any of the numbers they give a property as to its value, they normally do not take into consideration market trends and are overly generous on value or under value on any property. The properties you find must have to been sold within a realistic amount of time for the current market trends. In other words in a fast changing market you do not want to use a sale that happened two years ago and in a stale market six months might not be enough time to give you a good enough price picture. Once you have all your properties lined up that you want to use as comps add them all up and divide by the number of properties. For example properties A, B, C and D sold for $200,000 + $225,000 + $215,000 + $205,000 will add up to $845,000, you divide that by the number of properties you are using(4) and this will give you a safe number of $211,250 and this is the properties rough value. If none of those properties have special features and yours does, you can add in extra money for those features. Your property has a pool and those do not, you can add a small amount of money into your price to find what your property may actually bring to the market. There are many scientific formulas and ways of do comps but by far this is the easiest. Do not trust other people who tell you the value of a property especially people from the sale sites, they will always give you misinformation.

While you are doing all this you must send a driver over to check the property or drive to it yourself. It is good to have some construction knowledge or for the driver to have this knowledge because you must quickly without going into the property come up with a number as to what it is going to cost to repair the property. The only way to legally enter the property is for there to be a person occupying the property and for them to let you into the house, which almost never happens. The person who goes to the property must check to see if the property is occupied by knocking on the door and asking that person if they are a renter or homeowner. Renters will tell you, owners get hostile because they see you as trying to stealing their house and they have been dealing with people knocking on their door for weeks asking about the sale of their residence. This will come into factor if you have to do an eviction of the tenant but could work to your advantage if they are a renter and you want to rent the property out. The purpose of driving the property is to get an idea how much you have to deduct from that estimated value. The driver will have to give an estimated idea of what the cost will be to get the property in shape to be appealing to the market. Checking the properties occupancy will let you know what it is going to take for you to take possession of the property. Let's say you decide it is going to cost $10,000 dollars to get the property in shape to sell and it is occupied but the home owner, who is willing to take a small cash settlement to leave the property (called cash for keys) in the amount of $3,000. If we use the previous example value of $211,250, you could pay no more than $198,250 on the property before losing money. You will also have to take into consideration real estate sales costs and your own profit margin to come up with a realistic price to be willing to spend.

The last thing you need to do is attempt to buy the property. Let's use the example value of $211,250 and let's say that after realist deductions you decided the property is worth spending up to $175,000 dollars. All of your homework tells you that the property will go to sale that day and it will have an opening bid of $123,642.27. You will have to go to the sales with the full amount you are willing to spend in a format of money that the auctioneer will accept. Even with all of this done you still may not win the property at auction. Other people may have another type of use for the property. If you want to sell it your number may be lower than someone who plans to rent it out. Another bidder may plan to be the end user of the property or even if they plan to sell the property but have come up with a different number then you did their number could win the auction. Do not be discouraged or get too attached to any property there will be more going to sale that day or another day.

Chapter 7

Requirements to Buy at Trustee Sales

Chapter 7   Requirements to buy at trustee sales

The requirements to buy at most trustee sales are minimal. Most people assume there are lots of requirements and that the auctioneers have all sorts of information to give out to the people that come to the sales. People assume the auctioneers are going to be promoting the sale of each property trying to get bids. When it comes down to it this is just not the case. Very few auctioneers want anything to do with the people that are at the sale. They normally want the absolute minimum required by their companies to get the job done. You need to bring, money, identification and anything you require for comfort.

Auctions and auctioneers require cash or cashier's check, typically made out to yourself so that you can sign the checks over. If they are made out to a company you work for they will require a letter of authorization and most times require it to be notarized. They will want a copy of the letter to give to the trust every time you purchase something. If you plan to buy more than one property bring multiple copies. Most auctioneers require that checks do not get stale, which means they normally will not accept checks older than 90 days old. Even if your checks do not have any sort of expiration date on them. Now I know I said cash but when it comes down to it if you bring cash to buy a property you are asking for trouble and most auctioneers do not want that kind of trouble. Even though the process allows cash most auctioneers in effort to protect themselves will refuse cash because the auctioneers do not bring safes and there is a real threat of being robbed when holding millions of dollars from all the properties that sold that day. Cashier's checks have less interest to a thief because they would have to be seen at a bank attempting to sign checks not in their name. A bank unfamiliar with this person will want the checks verified by the issuing bank and proper identification with the ability to sign those checks before depositing or tendering cash on large checks.

At the beginning of any sale each auctioneer will want to see your funds and your identification. If you plan to bid you have to do this, it is called qualifying, you have to do it to prove that you can bid what you call out to the auctioneer and if they do not think you have as much as you are calling out as a bid, they will stop and check the paper they wrote the qualifications on. Your id will prove that you are the person on whose name is on the checks and if the checks are made to a company, your letter of authorization will show you are able to sign those checks as a signer for the company. Once you build a reputation as a bidder and the auctioneer learns who you are they will just want to see your checks. There is another type of trustee auction that does a preregistration before the auctions start. These auctions will not know if you over bid your checks but be aware it is illegal to bid more money than you have and you are ultimately responsible for that money. You can be arrested for not having the funds you say you do by bidding over your number. It is also illegal to bid on a property and not turn over the funds required for the purchase of the property, at the conclusion of the sale. If you make a mistake it is your problem and you must pay for the property. If an auctioneer forgives a mistake and allows you walk away, you may never be allowed to buy from that auctioneer again.

Most but not all trustee auctions are held outside and do not provide any creature comforts. You should bring something to sit on, clothes that prepare you for the type of weather expected for the day and something to eat because even indoor sales run long and do not provide food. In most instances you can find a restaurant in the area but sales, in some states, can be up to an eight hour day. Even bringing a snack is recommended especially if you have health issues.

The best advice for how to deal with any auctioneer is not to piss them off. Do not try to be their friend, which is different than being friendly. Auctioneers are under a great amount of stress from their offices and during busy times can work very long hours. A lot of auctioneers are grumpy and have the way they like things to get done. Just do them they are not doing anything that consists of breaking the law. Within their years of experience different things have happened and any the quirks they develop are generally because of that. Also everyone for some reason thinks the auctioneer is cheating and because auctioneers do not want to lose their jobs, they normally are not doing anything wrong. Because of that they get reported to the companies they work for often by distrusting investment companies and bidders, and sometimes to the federal government. It is important to remember as an investor that your investment will make you a lot of money fast. They have to grind to get that same amount over time and think everyone at sales is entitled, even when the bidders are people working for investors. If you want to buy at trustee sales often and have a long career in the business just smile and go with the flow.

Chapter 8
How to Bid

Chapter 8   How to bid

At most trustee sales you must verbally make a bid. Some types of auctions require you to raise a card or make some sort of gesture, like you see on TV. This is done to confuse you in the frenzy of bidding so you possibly make a wrong move or bid over your number. They also use many other tactics to confuse and throw you off your game, such as loud speakers with continuous talking, a tone from the auctioneer in his speech and frantic bid assistants that need that next bid. All of these things are done to try to get higher bids and take advantage of people that don't know any better. Most auctions require that you to say a bid higher than the last highest bid acknowledged and do not use the tactics from the cattle style auctions. Just be aware what type of auction it is before you get your money involved and be prepared to deal with either style.

Let's use this example, you are at a normal style auction, trustee sale, you have qualified with the auctioneer. You plan to bid on the next property being offered to sale by the crier, auctioneers are also called criers because they cry the sales, and he/she has acknowledgement that you are planning to bid. The auctioneer opens the sale at $121,472.34 and you plan to bid up to $175,000. The first customary thing to do is to offer the auctioneer a penny over. What this means is you will spend .01 cent over the opening asking price for the property being offered. Sometimes but not always the property will get no further bids and you will win the property for a lot less then what you were willing to spend. This is a blessing and a curse, you always feel like you got something great for cheap and then realize it is a possibility you missed something in your homework and might have just bought a really bad deal. Do not worry about it for too long there is more work to do whether at sales or at your office.

Going back to the last example, let's say there were five other people bidding on the property. Normally two of those five will have a tendency to take the lead. Others will come into the bidding and fall out along the way. Just remember to keep to your number there is no reason to push over it unless you are trying to push a competitor on a higher price for the property, which can be dangerous. Bidding is not complicated but if you have never done it, it will raise your heart rate and make you give off tells. When I say tells I mean just like in poker and if you show them most people who do this all the time can read them. The bidding goes back and forth, crosses over your $175,000 max price and keeps right on going. Let it, you did your job, played the game how you wanted to play it nothing was lost in the process and there are more properties waiting around the corner.

By law there is no minimum required amount to bid and anything higher than the last bid could be acknowledged but to save time auctioneers normally ask that you bid no less the $100.00 bids, some will have their own minimums. Sometimes if the opening bid and the approx value have a huge spread they will ask for higher amounts. For example bid opens a $100.00 and everyone knows the thing is worth over $500,000 it could take hours to get to that number by $100 bids so the auctioneer may ask for $1,000 minimum bids and sometime they will say until the bidding starts to slow down or it will be implied. Remember you are in their world you play by their rules and even though they seem unfair, they know the laws better then you do in most cases. Even if they do not have any other sales for the day and there are many hours left in the day for you, you must do as they ask. Making a big deal about it will just hurt you in the long run.

A lot of TV shows are showing auctions as part of the flipping process. Please remember TV is not real. Most of the auctions on those shows are faked and done for the process of making television. The people bidding have already won those properties at earlier sales or bought them through some other purchasing processes. Auctions are often shown on the lawn of a property on TV and auctions are allowed to be held at any public place. The lawn of the house can be used as a place of sale but in most cases is not where the auctions are conducted. The auction companies normally use a common place where multiple properties can be sold. It is rare for a company to sell it on the lawn. It is rare for the drivers to all go to one property at the same time during a sale. Then talk badly to each other, still standing at the property, while throwing bids to someone at the sales, by phone. Those properties are already owned by the people who win the auction and in some cases have already been remodeled. It is all done for TV and real sales can be quite boring. It does not make for good television to show someone in an office talking to someone at the sale on a phone, the fake conflict gets people to watch their show.

Chapter 9

Strategies for Bidding

Chapter 9   Strategies for bidding

Now that you know how to bid, we need to learn how to bid right. You need to know how to keep your opponents guessing to do this you need to, change up your bid amounts, watch your body language, keep your poker face on and do not leak important information. Your bidding and your competitions bidding has a lot to do with how you bid. This is a lot like a very expensive game of poker where if you do it wrong it will cost you or a company you work for thousands. Once you attend a sale you will see a lot of things that seem confusing hopefully we can minimize some of that.

As you will see most people at sale, especially people that work for companies will be on phones and making bids starting larger and descending. The people on the other end of phones are telling them what to bid, when to bid and what their max bid is. Ignore all of that, what you are concerned with is the amount of the bid. Normally bidders will start out the gate strong using larger number until they get closer to their max spending price then they get closer to the hundred dollar bid. Each player has their own strategy but you will see descending increments more often than not. It is important for you to change up the amount that you say and often, it keeps anyone from trying to read what you are doing. If you have a larger window to your maximum bid amount, throwing a larger bid is ok and sometimes shakes smaller maximum bid people off the property. If someone places the penny bid and you throw a much larger bid this is called slamming the bid, it is meant to shake as many people as possible. It works only when you do not have experienced players bidding but it is good to shake a few people off your property. Normally people bidding for others have to get their offices to notice what just happened, this delay can throw them off and smaller players or newer players, just lock up when they hear the large number. Besides slamming a bid just remember to change the bid amounts around do not do, $5,000's, $1,000's, $500's, $100's and oops I'm out of money. They can all see your hand if you do that and the idea is for them to not know what you are doing.

Inexperienced bidders have a tendency to get excited, their hearts beat fast, their hand shake and they love to do the pee-pee dance when they get close to their number. It is called the pee-pee dance because they step around from foot to foot in a dancing motion. It comes from excitement and the nervousness of winning or losing the property. You have to watch your body language it tells a lot about what you are doing. A pee-pee dancer will be telling you they are almost out of money. Someone who's hands are shaking just tells you they are new but it will also tell you, that you might be able to shake them off the property. Especially if their bid increment has decreased and you know you have room to go in your amount. Do not do things like cross your arms or stand in defensive postures, this shows you are not happy with the way the sale is going and means you are already paying more then you want to. A competitor will stick you with it if you do that. Being loud and intimidating will only works against weak people but having strength to your voice does not hurt your case. Authoritative people instinctively make others back down.

Your facial features will give off the same tells, as in poker, you have to watch how you carry your expressions as you bid. One of the weakest things you can do I look over at the person who just placed a bid. It tells them that you are trying to read them, you are about out of money and you do not know your next safe move. Making disgusted expressions, making happy expressions and looking around, all tell people things and you are not trying to tell anyone anything. The best thing you can do is keep your eyes on the auctioneer and keep your interactions with others to a minimum.

As you get comfortable at sales you will find people to interact with, some may buy in your area and some may not, either way, watch what you say. Treat being at sales like the walls have eyes and ears. Even people you become friendly with can ask you things in just the right way to gain information from you. If they are just making conversation everyone within ear shot can hear it and will. If the people who hear it do not care they will tell someone who will. Watch what you say it can easily come back to bite you. It is also important to know that you can not make a deal with anyone to try to acquire a property for less money than it could possibly get through the auction process. This is called bid chilling and collusion, it is illegal and you could get jail time for doing it. If someone comes up and offers you money to not bid on a property or offers a partnership on the property to keep you out of the bidding and you agree to it. You are colluding and sometimes government representatives are at sales to try to catch people doing this. If someone is interested in a partnership it is not illegal to enter into one but you should not be making those deals at the sales site it can be read as an attempt to chill the bid. Be responsible at the sales site and you will not have any problems.

Chapter 10

What Happens Next/ Where do I Get My Keys?

Chapter 10   What happens next/ Where do I get my keys?

One of the funniest questions you will hear after someone buys a property at a trustee sale is, "where do I pick up my keys?". The answer is there aren't any keys, you have to figure out how to get into your own property. Most people send a locksmith to change the locks or if you have the skill to work a drill and change a lock, you do it yourself. What really happens when you win your property is you do paperwork. Nothing overly complicated but you must fill out a receipt of purchase, with your vesting or how you want to hold title, then you get a deed and record it. Not every state does their sales this way but this is one of the most common ways the process happens. Each thing is easy to understand but there are some things you need to know.

The bidding has concluded and you are the highest bid for the property. Next thing to do is give the auctioneer your checks for the property. Generally signed and endorsed over to the trustee but the auctioneer will help you with how they want the checks, if you have never done it before. Some states only require a deposit of up 10% of the purchase price and the rest of the funds to be turned over within 24 to 48 hours. Most state require all the funds at the conclusion of the sale and some auctioneers will wait until they have a break in sales to do all the paperwork to make sure you do not mess it up.

The paperwork is simple, it normally has information on it pertaining to you. To make sure you didn't give them bad checks and to make sure they can get all your paperwork back to you, such as title information and refund. The questions are things like name, address, phone number, company you work for, owner of the property, your position in the company, check information (check numbers and amount), drivers license number, sign it, date it and (most important) vesting. The vesting has to be reported back and soon as the auctioneer gets a chance to send it in. The trustee's want this information as soon as they can get it, so they know which properties to start prepping the paperwork for because they will no longer be owned by them or the bank. Remember most trustees are the bank but either way they have paperwork that needs to happen so they need the information fast. The auction company appointed by the trust will call or email it in to their office and they will send it into the trustee's office or the bank.

Vesting is how you hold title which means what you want it to say on the deed. I will not tell anyone how to hold title but I will give you some examples:

"John Smith as his sole and separate property"

This just means John Smith is the only person responsible for anything on the title at the time of the sale until he sells it.

"John Smith and Jane Smith as joint tenants"

This means the couple holds title together and are both responsible for the title

"John Smith as 30% owner, Joseph Johnson as 30% owner, Kenneth R. Thomas as 30% owner and Daniel Williams as 10% owner in partnership"

This means they all own the property and all are responsible for the title but it does not say anything about if they live there. The percentages show how much liability each should be given and also helps each figure out how much they have to pay for their part of property repairs. This is a common vesting at sales for investor groups.

"The state street trust #1234 6/8/10 Jim's Investment Company INC. as trustee"

This is not the most common vesting but is written this way to make sure liability only happens from the date of purchase and gives a corporation the ability to hold the title since in the eyes of the law a corporation is a living entity. It also releases any person from the liability unless they are a managing member of the corporation. The street address is represented backwards so you know what trust it is and which one of the properties on that street by making the address numbers look like an inventory numbers. This is vesting into a trust and again is not common but a good example of overly complicated vesting. Your vesting should be written clearly and neatly because this is the way it will be written on your deed. Eventually how you will record your deed and you want it to make sense or it could look like it is someone else's property. If someone else attempted to lay claim to your property it could cost a lot of money in court.

Once your paperwork is done all that is left to do is wait. Your deed and any possible refund will come in the mail in anywhere from a week to two weeks after you bought the property. Once you have your deed in hand you need to record it. This means take your deed to the county recorder's office and have it recorded into the chain of title. This will further protect your rights on the land and make any case in court stronger. It is important to record your deed as soon as possible to prevent someone from recording a fraudulent deed in its place. This is not common thing but is possible and could be disproved in court but then who wants to fight a court battle like that, when you know the property is yours. In other words record your deed!

The last thing I will mention on this topic is your rights to the property begin when you buy the property. If it is not occupied you can go into the property the day you buy it and change the locks to prevent someone else from squatting on your land. If it is occupied you have rights to the land but can not enter the property. You need to work out something with the renter or previous owner if you want to see the inside of the property. The previous owner is also responsible for rent if they still occupy the property, the entire time they occupy the property but that is an issue that has to be settled in court and normally these judgments do not get paid.

Section 4

Occupancy and Renting

Chapter 11

Leaving Tenants in Place and Renting

Chapter 11   Leaving tenants in place and renting

Now that you own a property lets use the example that it is occupied and you planned to rent the property out. Sometimes the previous owner will be interested in renting back the property and sometimes the people in the house are tenants of the previous owner. You should have figured out through all of your homework how much you plan to charge for rent on the property, which will tell you if they can afford to rent it back from you. If the previous renters have an existing lease in most cases you must honor the lease, until the leases term or you prove the lease to be faulty or fraudulent. If the occupant is the previous owner they may not be able to move because of many things and leasing the property they use to own may fix the situation for them. The first thing you have to do is talk to them to find out what their situation is whether they are renter or owner and if they plan to leave. This should have been done before you purchased the property.

The property is occupied by the previous owner of the property and they plan to leave as soon as their apartment is ready in a few day. Great now you can put the property on the rental market and rent it out. This can be done fairly easily, you need pictures of the property and to find an online or written publication that rents out properties. Write a short description of what the property is and add in your pictures. You can put up your asking price or leave it off depending on what you are attempting to accomplish. You also need to set up a rental agreement whether it is a month to month rental or a lease for a term. These terms just mean an agreement to rent the property for six months or more. The most common leases are normally a year or two on a residence. The leasing agreement will protect you and them in case the lease is to be broken and will spell out the things you want done such as security deposit, first and last, cleaning fee, credit check and background checks. If you do not feel comfortable with writing a rental agreement, most office supply store sell generic forms and they can be found online. Be careful to read any form you expect someone to sign because they are legally bidding and if it has stipulations in it you do not agree to then it is not a form you want to use.

You want to rent the property out but you do not feel like doing all the work to rent it. You can find many property management companies in your area that offer the service of finding renters for properties. A property management company will market your property to potential renters and show the properties for you. They will also offer rental agreements that protect them from any liability on the rental and they can addend them to put in things you want. A property management company normally charges a monthly fee for this. It can be anywhere from 10%-50% of the monthly rent and the percentage depends on the income of the area and location of the property. It is smart to shop around and get the most amount of information possible about their services including rental rates for the area and how much they charge before making a decision on one. They will generally collect the rent also, to make sure they get their money straight off the top and send you a check for the remainder. They can also field all of the service calls on the property for you and will ask you if you want to fix it or if you want them to send out a repairman. The repairman will sometimes work for them and send a bill to you for the services done on the property or it will be deducted from your check for the rent. This service makes life much easier for the owner of the property but remember to figure that into your equation when figuring out what you want to pay for the property.

If the people who are occupying your new venture are the renters of the previous owner, have them show you their lease. Take a picture or make a copy of it for your records. This document now becomes important to you. It is also important to know that any security deposit that was given by the renter is now your responsibility. It is still owed by the previous owner of the property to you but in most cases you will have to take the previous owner to small claims court and a judgment can be granted by the judge but if they did not have money to pay the mortgage, they will not normally pay you the deposit even with a judgment against them. When the time comes for the renter to leave it will almost always come out of your pocket. You first need to determine if the lease is a real lease, most renters will not know what a lease looks like and what should be written in a lease. If the previous owner gave them a lease within the time of the foreclosure it can be determined by a court that is was done to further lock up what is now your property. If that is proven the renters can be evicted for a faulty lease. Otherwise if it says they pay $500.00 a month less then you wanted to get for the property and it is a valid lease you have to honor the lease until its term and evict them after the leasing term. The other way to get them out is to show they are not paying the lease at all or have done vandalism to your property which all has to be valid and provable in court. It is also important to know that during the Obama administration renter rights have been extended to cover a lot more things. Make sure to read up on all of the rules that protect renters and do harm to landlords.

I did not go into details on if the occupant is the previous owner and refuses to move because that will be covered in detail in the next chapter. It is not as simple as asking them to leave and having them pack their stuff and leaving. This is why it is important to talk to the occupants residing there before you purchase the property.

Chapter 12

Cash for Keys and Evictions

Chapter 12   Cash for keys and evictions

Your property is occupied by someone who does not plan to leave. After talking to them they say their new place will not be ready for a few months. This is the simplest of examples I can explain. Offer to rent them the property for the short term, on a month to month basis, they plan to be in the there and get it in writing and signed by them. Otherwise you will have no legal recourse when they refuse to pay or do not want to leave.

You have people in your property that refuse to leave, the best you can do is offer them what is called, cash for keys. You offer them a short amount of time to move their stuff out of the property with a cash boot that will be given when they turn over the keys. This has become so common place most people who have been through a foreclosure know about it and will expect you to offer it. You must also get them to sign something showing they have agreed to it and then have them sign another document when they turn over the keys showing they are officially done with you and your property. This just gives you as the owner a chain of events in writing if it ends up in court. The cash offered is generally around $1,000-$5,000 depending on the area. This is a fairly easy way to remove an unwanted occupant as well but some companies and investor refuse to pay cash for keys. This course of action becomes a game of attrition or who will end the battle first. Companies that do this all the time have a team of lawyers ready to drop all the legal action possible on the occupants and it is not recommended if you just do not have the cash to spare for a cash for keys deal. If you try to stick to your guns on not paying cash for keys you could be stuck in a lengthy court battle.

You walk up to the door of your new property and are met by an angry person holding a weapon, screaming at you to leave their property at once. Often times it does not get this ugly but this is about the worst case scenario. At this point it is time to start the legal eviction process.

For purposes of making this simple, I will explain the step required because the times required are different in different states. Also the Obama administration has changed the laws to protect renters and a lot of those rules are still in effect, it is important to read up on what changes affect you. The first document you need is an eviction notice, it is generally called a, 3 day notice to pay or quit but in your case you just need them out. Once the notice has expired you need to file with court system what is called an unlawful detainer. This document tells the court and the occupant you have filed a complaint with the court, to reacquire your real estate. This does not give you the right to go into the property and it has its own amount of time that has to be followed before you can file for the next document. Which is called a writ of possession, this document gives you the court appointed power to have them removed from the property. You generally have to speak with the police in your area to execute the document especially when the occupant is hostile. A police officer will accompany you to escort the occupant off your property and give you time to change the locks. Often times an occupant that did not want to leave will attempt to return. It is always wise to have someone guard your property to make sure they do not break back into the property or they will be considered a new squatter and the process will start over again. The previous owners have an allotted amount of time to come back for their belongings even if the property was vacant from an occupant or occupied by someone. Generally any personal property over $500.00 must be kept safe for the previous owner for up to 90 days. If the occupant was hostile or not even there when you took possession, do not let them into the property. You most go in and get the things they ask for or they could refuse to leave if you allow them inside. This person could become a squatter, which you would again have to evict and the process is not anything you want to go through twice. The eviction process itself can take up to 6 months or more if the occupant has legal representation or a good knowledge of the laws.

Chapter 13
No Occupant

Chapter 13   No occupant

If there is no one living in your new property there is very little to worry about. Drill the old lock out and put your new lock in its place. Secure all the doors and windows and look for places that could be break in points and secure them better. A squatter can become as invasive as a previous owner and vandals will destroy and steal things while you are not there. Also make sure to visit your property often and place a notice in a window or on a door telling neighbors the house is privately owned so they know to call the police if they see people inside. It is also smart to talk to the immediate neighbors in the area and let them know you now own the property. Some people like the window shades open to show the neighbors it is empty and some like them closed to detour vandals and squatters. If the previous owner has left personal property behind it is required that you keep the property for an amount of time determined by each state if that property is in excess of a certain dollar amount. Otherwise it is now yours to rent or sell how you please.

Section 5

Repairing Your Property

Chapter 14

Self Fixer Upper vs. Contractor

Chapter 14 Self fixer upper vs. contractor

Now that you have a vacant property you have to evaluate if you want to fix it yourself. You should have some knowledge of construction and property inspections before walking through the property. You also should have some preliminary numbers of what you estimated the cost of repair to be before entering the property. While inside you need to inspect everything and be able to estimate the actual costs. If the jobs contained in the property are bigger than your experience covers it is a good idea to hire a contractor or handyman to make the repairs. This all depends on the type of work required. You would not hire a contractor to hang your mini-blinds, it is just too small of a job for a contractor in most situations and requires no permits to do the job. A large investment firm would have the infrastructure set up already and they would send out their own construction crews to deal with the property. We are looking at this from a first time stand point and do not have such people on payroll.

It is not required that you have permits in most areas to do minor improvements to your property. You should have a good working knowledge of the laws for your area before starting any construction. You should also have some experience with construction if you plan to do all or some of the work yourself. It can be helpful to have a general contractor's license when attempting to start a project like this because it will give you enough knowledge to know what requires permits and what does not. If you start a project that requires permits and an inspector shows up on your property you could be given a red tag on your property. Red tags can cause the property to be uninhabitable without proper corrections made as soon as possible which would mean you would have to bring in a contractor, pull the correct permits and get permission from the city to reenter the property to make those corrections. A lot of times properties need things like, light bulbs, appliances, new landscaping, paint and carpet which none of these things require permits to be done most of the time because they are consider things any home owner would do.

Any inspection done by you to evaluate costs of repair should include anything and everything on the property. You should check all the switches and outlets, with the power turned on to the house, for proper operation. You should check all appliances and fixtures such as toilets and tubs. You should also check for termite and mold damage around the house and in the attic spaces. The attic will tell you if the roof is leaking and in need of being repaired along with being able to check for illegal wiring. People do not like to be in attics and crawl spaces so a lot of repair work done in these places is done poorly. The house also needs to have curb appeal you may have to change landscaping or paint the house to make it more desirable. On the inside of a property the house has to feel warm and inviting and follow current trends but still be generic enough that a person feels like they could make it into their own. If a room has paneling no one will be interested in it because paneling was popular in the 70's. Remember that when looking at the interior of a house. Brass fixtures are not a current trend and are found in many homes because it was popular for so long. This will have to be changed to something more in style if you want to make the property marketable. Everything needs to work, everything needs to look appealing and everything needs to be functionally sound. As the owner of the property you are held liable for the house for up to 1 year after it is sold, in most states, and if the damage is found to be pre-existing you will have to pay for the repairs, even if the property is sold as is.

If you have no construction, home repair or inspection experience it is probably better to hire a contractor. Contractors will be able to make the necessary inspections to tell you what is required to get the house in shape and you will have to tell them what you want done to make it marketable. Contractors take each job required and input their cost for material, employee time and profit for the company. If you want to see what each job is going to cost you have to ask for a line item bid. Contractor do not like to give them because often times people will approve some items and reject others for a different contractor to come in and make those repairs. Hiring multiple contractors is not recommended because they will increase the cost of each item feeling that they will be held responsible for the other contractor's supervision. They will also increase the costs for their extra time to write a long bid and they see it as, you asking for explanation on each item, slowing down their process of getting the job done. Contractors like to write the general items you want done and the price. This is the most common way a bid will come from a contractor. It is smart to shop around for a contractor until you get what you want from the work being done. It is also good to try a few out if you plan to do many of these types of projects.

Just so you have a basis of understanding, a large company who does this on a regular basis will most times be able to do construction cheaper than a person hiring a contractor. Large companies hire teams of people that work on their properties on a regular basis. The prices they pay are the cost for the people working plus the cost of materials. The only way to get a cheaper price is to do it yourself. If you have the knowledge to complete most of the jobs required on a property, the price you pay for the property can be closer to market value because you are doing the work. It is wise to have at least enough knowledge to inspect the property and know what you are paying for when it comes to repairs.

Chapter 15

Things Always Fixed

Chapter 15 Things always fixed

Unless you purchased a property that was just remodeled to be placed on the market by the previous owner there are things in the property that will need to be replaced and/or repaired to make it marketable or rentable. When looking at the interior and the exterior of the property you need to take your personal feeling out of the equation. Some things done to a property just throw prospective buyers off your property when first looking at it. You want your property to make a good first impression and then be able to keep their interest until they decide to make an offer.

You almost always need to paint the exterior of a house fresh paint gives a house a fresh feeling. People walking up to the property will want to see clean looking walls as they approach the house. You will also have to clean the yard and/or hire landscaping people to freshen up the yard. You also need to make sure the grass looks good, even if the grass is in good shape you need to fix any dead spots and make sure the sprinklers work properly. You can not be there all the time and you want to make sure the lawn get watered. Any fences falling down or gates not working need to be repaired and possibly painted if the old wood or paint doesn't match the rest of the house. Also clean cob webs off of window frames and eves, even if they just happened. It makes the place seem empty and dirty before they have even got to see the inside. If you do not paint the house you must paint the door. The door is the first part of the house people interact with and if it is dirty or does not work properly it will start to raise doubts at the beginning.

The interior of the property needs to be painted as well. If you were told it was painted recently you need to evaluate the paint for finger prints and dirty marks, these are signs you need to paint. You need to pull all the old nails from the walls, where the previous owner's hung their pictures. Your potential buyers do not want to think, "Oh, that's where the picture goes.", they want to have the feeling they get to set up the house. Nail holes need to be filled and painted to cover them up. Carpet is disgusting and it needs to be replaced, the previous owners pet may have marked it or spills may have occurred. You do this for two reasons, it gives the house a smell of fresh carpet, which may smell bad but is a sign of repair. It shows potential buyers you put money into the house and carpet can be relatively cheap. The other reason is to make the house generic, people like to see properties with a somewhat generic set up it gives them the feeling they can improve it and make it their own. Besides no one want to see green shag when they walk through the door, typically a tan carpet is the cheapest and most common style used.

You also need to make sure all the appliances and fixtures work properly. Change any burned out light bulbs, sometimes people come after dark to see a house and you want all built in light fixtures to turn on without fail. You also need to remove any odd improvements from the previous owner, like a screen door in the hallway. You do not want people walking through the property to ask themselves, "What's this for?". It is a red flag that will make them think the house is odd.

Any prospective buyer needs to see your property and think this is nice and then walk through the property and continue to feel that way. You also want them to feel like they could live there and this is done by letting them think they could make minor changes and to make it feel like this is their home. When a person is done walking through it they need to remember it after walking through a few other properties that day. It needs to stay in their mind long enough to go back to their real estate agents office and write an offer. These minor improvements almost always are ones that help drive your house into a potential buyer's minds.

Chapter 16

Things Sometimes Fixed

Chapter 16   Things sometimes fixed

Beyond the list of things always fixed are the things sometimes fixed. These are not necessarily expensive things but normally are more expensive. Appliances are an example of these expensive repairs especially when you have to replace them all. Generally these are the things caused by vandalism or lack of use of an abandoned property. These are all the things that do not directly affect the look of the house, but they can, and are essential to having a house that can be lived in.

Looking at the appliances there are many reasons to change them, they are out dated, do not work or are miss matched. It is good to create a relationship with vendors who can supply these because if you plan to do this more than once you will buy a lot of appliance. Appliances can change the feel of a kitchen and if your appliances are out dated your remodeled house will feel like it has a kitchen from the 70's. Remember people like to play with things as they walk through the house, people will turn on appliances just to see if they like how they function. Garbage disposals are a great example people love to flick that switch to see what it does and if the garbage disposal does not turn on, it becomes a discouraging item. If a property had been vacant for a long time garbage disposals freeze up and need to be replaced. This is a relatively cheap way to keep a possible buyer happy as they venture through your property.

Fixtures have the same affect on people and sometimes they need to be changed, brass is very common on doors, bathrooms, kitchens and lighting fixtures but is not currently a trending style. This style went out in the early 90's and unless you plan to market the property to an older couple it is wise to update to a brushed nickel, brushed chrome or something closer to a silver color. Replacing fixtures can cost as much as all the appliances if you have a lot of brass to clear off. Brass is not the only reason to replace fixtures, a fresh remodel will make older fixtures look old and trashy.

Some of the time they just do not work, previous owners do not always replace broken items because it is just too much money and a hassle. You will have to change them or fix them, people will want it to turn on. Showing a house where the power, water and gas are not on is not advisable either. You might be trying to avoid people seeing broken things but if they do not find it an inspector will and that will cause you to either have to fix it or lose a buyer because of the fight over who will fix it.

Vandals have a tendency to destroy anything and everything. It is important to inspect a property thoroughly when you suspect vandalism. People generally kids will break things just to break them and previous owners who were evicted will also. A common thing to see is holes punched in walls or spray painting on the interior. These are things you did not want to repair but it must be done if you want someone to be a serious buyer of your property. Even when a person is looking to buy a fixer upper, they have no intention of fixing that kind of damage unless you expect them to pay almost nothing for the house. Previous owners sometimes do very serious damage to the house. One of the worst examples of this is concrete in the sewer drains. It is a costly repair and a property can not be re-sold without properly working drains in the house. When a person buys a new property it is required that some things work. A working toilet is one of those things if the drains are clogged with concrete a toilet will not flush. This could possibly cause the property to be red tagged or condemned by the city.

A house that has been abandoned for a long period of time will have many little bugs wrong with it. Houses like to be lived in and when things do not get used they break. The garbage disposal was one example of this, they seize up when they have not been used in a long time. This can sometimes be a quick fix by manually turning the motor, from the bottom of the unit, but most of the time the damage is done and it has to be replaced. The bathroom fixtures are also examples of this. Toilet lines, sink lines and toilet seals will all dry out and leak from the water being turned off for a long period of time. It is often a good idea to replace these because the leaks do not always show up right away. This means right about the time people are walking through your property they will spot water on the floor or hear toilets running from these types of problems.

Electrical outlets are a common example of something sometimes changed. People love to customize their house over time. People often change outlets or outlet plate covers. People walking through your property will not want to see the cartoon animal switch cover plate in what use to be a kids room. You do not know what they plan to use the room for, the last thing you want to do is lock in their mind that this room is used for a specific type of person, in this case a child's room. Most people want to see plain white outlets and plain white covers. It is a good idea to standardize all of the outlets and/or change them all if they are out dated. Most people do not know but older houses came with 2 prong outlets and no grounding system in a house, besides the electrical panel. It is important to update them to a 3 prong style and ground each outlet to its box. This will create a grounding system and reduce any possible fire hazard. A property inspector can also require this to be done again because it can be considered a fire hazard.

The things you sometimes change are the things you do not always see, they are often times hidden but important none the less. You need to also take some of these things into consideration as you are coming up with a number to pay for the property. You can always expect that some of these things will have to be done if you look at them from an educated stand point. There would be no way to know a water heater needs replaced but if you have a house built in 1955 you can expect the outlets will need updated. If a previous owner did it for you, you might have to use that money for an outdated water heater. Sometimes you get lucky and that extra money will go back into your pocket rather than towards more repairs.

Chapter 17

Things Never Fixed

Chapter 17   Things never fixed

This title for this chapter is impossible, there is never any one thing that is not changed, fixed or repaired. It is impossible to carry the expectation you will never have to repair any specific thing. Each property is different and sometimes you have to fix or repair the one thing you have never had to in the past. The idea is better expressed as, the things you would rarely ever have to fix but that doesn't make for a good title and doesn't really get the point across as quickly. Here we will deal with those things and I will give a great example of why sometimes those things have to be replaced.

A property is going to sale, you did your homework and you drove to the property the morning of the sale. You saw it was not occupied and in ok shape. You did your numbers on the property and the bid comes out low. You qualified with the auctioneer and no one else did. You bid offering a penny over no one else bids.

You are amazed you got it so cheap but carry on doing your receipt. As you walk away from the auctioneer someone comes up and says, "hey, didn't you hear that some homeless squatter burned that thing down this morning!" You just bought a burned out property. You own land that you paid too much money for and the whole house has to be replaced to get it back on the market. You have two options, sell the land and take a big loss or rebuild a house and take a smaller loss for a greater investment. If the best option is to rebuild a house than you are going to replace everything, which means there is always a situation where something you did not expect to replace, has to be replaced. This is just an example but a person unknowingly buying burned out properties is much more common than you would think. If this happens to a smaller company it could cause that company to go under. Larger companies can deal with the loss but are not happy about it happening and people generally get fired over it.

Now that we know it can happen, let's look at those things that are repaired and fixed less often than most. A great example of something you rarely do is a room addition as attractive as extra rooms are it is less likely the addition will bring the extra value for the money you spent. It does happen in instances where you can quickly throw up a wall in the space of an open den and create an extra bedroom quickly. Knocking down walls and expanding out to gain extra space, is expensive and the extra costs do not bring increased price from the market in most areas. It is one of those things that are rarely done in the flipping market. It can be done if you have a high value area with an old small square footage property on large land. This is not as uncommon in those areas but you are more likely to see the house replaced for an apartment building.

Concrete is an area that is less commonly replaced, the house sits on concrete and pools are made out of a form of concrete. Concrete quickly becomes an expensive venture and most flippers try not to get into replacing it if they do not have to. Concrete foundations and slabs can crack which is common but when inspecting, or an inspector is inspecting. They look for sinking cracks in the slab. This is a sign that the ground below the house is not compacted properly and that part of the house is sinking into the ground. It will also show as cracks in the walls and an uneven roof pitch, these things are normally all together. Pools where a property is unoccupied sometimes get emptied out. This is not good in some areas, the water can actually be holding the concrete down, and with pools the concrete is actually called gunite which is spray form of concrete used for pools. What will happen is when the water has been emptied out of the pool, the pool will pop out of the ground over time. The only real fix for this problem is to jack hammer out the old pool and replace it or fill the pool in with dirt and concrete, possibly lowering the value of your property.

There are many other things that you will find over time that do not get replaced, on a flipped property, but these are just a few examples of some of the more expensive one. When looking over a property that you plan to buy at trustee sale there is no way to account for these possible repairs. The only way to find these problems before purchasing a property, is buying it through the MLS and walking through the property. A traditional sale gives you the advantage of finding these kinds of problems before and possibly not having to pay for the repairs. If the previous owner is willing to do them to keep more money in the deal it is to your advantage and sometimes they will be willing to sell the house at a lower cost if you are willing to deal with the repairs. Without looking at the property there is no real way to account for the cost of such repairs until you find them after you have purchased the property.

Section 6

Moving Your Investment/ Selling

Chapter 18

Selling Your Investment Property

Chapter 18   Selling your investment property

You now have a remodeled property and you do not plan to rent it out. You need to put it on the market. As with buying properties you have some options. You can sell it yourself if you are an agent or broker. You can also hire an agent to sell it for you to avoid the hassle that comes with selling it yourself. If you have a larger company with its own brokerage you can have one of your agents do it for you. Selling it yourself has some things that go into the process that you need to do if you want to attract buyers.

If you plan to sell the property yourself, you must be an agent working for a brokerage. Otherwise your license is not valid and you could get in trouble with the DRE for working as an agent outside of an agency. Oddly though it is not required that you be an agent to sell a property. You can sell the property as an owner seller but your ability to market the property is much more limited. It requires knowledge of the paperwork to sell the property or the agent for the buyer could take advantage of you without you understanding what you did. Your brokerage will be able to market your property to other agents and potential buyers. Being with an agency gives you the ability to place the property on the local MLS. This will allow all the agents and brokers in the area to be able to see the property is available and go visit the property with potential buyers. Marketing the property to potential buyers and not having to pay an agent fees are the main advantage to doing your sale this way.

If you have no interest in becoming an agent or broker the best way to sell the property is to hire an agent. An agent will be able to do the marketing of your property to the public and to others agents. This includes listing your property on the MLS, placing ads with the property in them and conducting open houses. If you take the risk of doing it yourself without an agent you will have no way to market the property except placing a sign on your lawn. Hiring an agent will cost you about

3% of the properties sale price and traditionally the seller pays the buyer's agent fees also. This normally works out to 6% in total. The costs can be steep but if you do not want to pay the buyer's agent fees you will not be able to sell the property in today's style of market.

An important thing to know about using an agent to sell your property is not to sign anything to hire your agent. A lot of agents want to make sure they get paid and will use an exclusive right to sell contract. If you sign any agreement with an agent you are basically agreeing to pay them. If in the event your property does not sell, you will be required to furnish the 3% to your agent if you sign a contract, this is what these contracts are designed for. The agent will keep records of their attempt to sell the property and if you reject offers close to the asking price they can require you pay them based on their due diligence and your unruliness. These also end up in court often because the agent feels that they did their job selling it and you were not willing to take a realistic offer on the property. Especially if you were willing to make counter offers on offers that were lower than the asking price. In other words a contract to sell a property can be dangerous for a seller and you should seek other options if you plan to sell your property.

If you own or work for a large company that does flips on a regular basis they will have the infrastructure in place to have an agent working for the company put the property on the market. Agents still want their 3% of the sale but your advantage here is your company is acting as the brokerage and you get to keep a portion of their 3% because you are their broker or your company is. If you work for the company they can allow you to use their agents but you will not get a part of the 3% back. You just have the advantage of knowing the agent and how they work. Unless you are the agent for the company than it is whatever deal you work out with your broker to sell your property.

The federal government and each state have different rules regarding lending money on flipped properties. A potential buyer may love your property but not be able to get a loan for the property if the flip has happened too quickly. Some states require ninety days and some require six months or more of ownership of the property before lending money on a flipped property. If you buy a property, it is in perfect shape needing no repair and you see a potential for profit by selling the property. Your property could end up on the market too fast, it is important to know what the rules in your area are for flipping. If the property gets offers and you accept one, your buyer might not be able to get the loan funded by a bank. There are some banks that specialize in flipped properties and their loan officers will know how to deal with the sale. They will know the minimum amount of time required in that area before the loan can be funded and may be able to wait out the term during the paperwork processing. A large bank can become uninterested in funding the loan because the rules from state to state are different and the loan officers often get lines crossed with other people working on the file in their own offices. Some banks will just flat out refuse to deal with the file. It is important to find a lender who you can offer to the buyer if their initial bank will not fund the loan. Most buyers will use the bank they normally do their banking through and those banks are less likely to want to deal with the loan. Your secondary option could end up saving the sale of your property. Without it your buyer could fall out of escrow and want their deposit back or cause other problems for you that you did not want to deal with. Especially if those problems end up in court and the person did not even buy your property.

It is also important to be aware of market types whether buying or selling a property. Real estate markets fluctuate on roughly a 7 year cycle. It is important to know if you are on an upswing or down swing in the market. Economic factors do play into the cycle of the market but does not directly affect the market, it functions on its own. The type of market you are in will directly affect the asking price and the types of offers you get on the property. In downward markets you will see offers come in under your asking price because the market is dropping and they feel they can get it cheaper than your asking price and probably get you to repair things that are not needed. In upward markets you will see offers come in above your asking price, even if the market will not sustain that price, and you are more likely to sell the property as is without making extra repairs. In a stale market prices will slowly increase or decrease but all the same things apply for an up or down market. It is important to understand what market you are in because it will affect your purchases and sales. It will affect your experience at a trustee sale and also bring in or drop certain players from the trustee sales. In a down market you will not want to spend as much on a property because it could drop in value before it is placed on the market. In an up market you could spend more for it if you factor the market will continue to go up. Getting caught in the shift from up to down market can cause a serious loss in money if you are not careful with your properties.

Chapter 19

Sorting Through the Offers

Chapter 19   Sorting through the offers

Your property has now been on the market and offers are starting to come in. It is always smart not to take the first offer. It may be the best offer but offers are good for a few days. You might see something else you like, better terms or more money. Depending on the type of market you are in will change the type of offers you get. You may also find none of the offers are what you wanted and you may have to change what you intended the property to be used for.

As offers start to come in remember to look through all of them. Agents will put things into the offers to protect themselves and the buyers they represent and some of those things may be detrimental to you. Most offers come in with what is called standard verbiage but sometimes experienced agents will put in things like time limits, rebates or commitments that are made because the buyer wanted certain things in the deal or have certain needs to purchase your property. These offers may be attractive but when you pencil out what it will cost it could be worse than taking an offer for less money.

If you are in a booming market and you put your property up for market value you could see offers for more than expected. In the same respect, in a falling market offers could come in for less than what you put it on the market for. In a booming or falling market it is important to realize that the appraisal may not come back with the number you were offered. If that number is less than the offer, the buyer will have to make up the difference in cash and the bank will not fund the entire purchase. If that number is higher you, as the seller, may get greedy and want to walk away from the accepted offer, it is not advisable to do so. You could end up in court with the buyer because you wanted to make a few thousand dollars more. The only safe way to walk away from a deal in this situation is if the buyer breaks the terms of the agreement by doing any number of things but exceeding due diligence time limits is a common way.

Sometimes things just do not work out the way you intended and you have to do something else with the property. If the offers that come in are not acceptable because they are so low you will lose money or any other reason where you could take a loss. Sometimes it is better to change what you planned to do with the property. If you are in a down market and the prices offered for the property are not going to cover your cost. It might be better to rent or lease the property. Basically after all is said and done, you got in over your head and can not sell it. Renting out the property gives you the option to make money on it while you wait for the value to exceed your investment, this is a common problem for first time investors. The market does not always sustain the values you think they do and it is important to be able to have a backup plan if this is your first time doing this. Overall lowering your risk to some extent, this is a dangerous world of investment and rookie mistakes can have serious consequences. The ability to have a backup plan at this point may be a newcomer's only saving grace.

Chapter 20

Escrow

Chapter 20   Escrow

Once you have selected an offer to accept on your property for sale. The property will go into escrow, which is a process you may have already been through if you bought your property through a traditional sale. Escrow is a process that is required on a sale even if the offer on the property is a cash offer. Escrow is a third party making sure you, as the seller, and the buyer complete all of the tasks required to close the sale in a timely fashion.

In your offer a specific escrow company will have been selected and agreed upon by both parties. The escrow company will be given the accepted offer and the deposits first before anything else. It is what is considered the start of escrow and is also the first day if you have an escrow that is required to end within a certain time frame. Escrows normally are 30, 60 or 90 days on most residences. Commercial real estate deals typically have longer escrow periods.

Once escrow has started each party will be sent preliminary documents as to the tasks required to complete escrow and have the loan for the buyer funded by the bank. For the buyer it is generally information required about them, where their money comes from, what insurance they want to carry on the property, if they want or require an impound account for the taxes, paying for inspections and other things of that nature. For the seller it is a little more leg work of setting up inspections, making repairs to the property and prepping the documentation on the house so it can be transfers to the new owner.

Once all of the tasks have been completed and the bank does not have issues with the deal. The escrow officer will order documents. These documents need to be signed with a notary public by the buyer and sent back to escrow. This will trigger the bank to release the funds for the sale and the closing paperwork will be sent out to each party involved.

Obviously this is a simple explanation of escrow because escrow is a tough process. Even though a third party is brought in to make the transition easy, on each party, it becomes complicated because of all the people and paperwork involved. When dealing with a flipped property the bank wants as much information as possible to make sure they do not give money on a bogus deal. As the seller it can become daunting dealing with the bank and all of their confused regulations on what they will fund the loan based on and their inability to decipher the laws. As the buyer getting the seller to make the required repairs so the loan will fund and making sure the inspections are completed in a timely manner can cause problems. Inspectors can cause problems finding issues neither party see as a problem. However your escrow goes, they almost never get closed on time and extending the time period of escrow at the beginning just gives escrow time to work on other files. It is important to keep on every party involved to make sure things happen in a realistic time frame. If you expect escrow to close in 30 days you should be willing to allow a week or two extra to give all the parties involved time to get their jobs done. A lot of the time it is not a buyer or a seller holding up the deal and you should take that into consideration before pulling the property out of escrow and waiting for a new buyer.

Section 7

Your Next Steps and Drawbacks

Chapter 21

Getting Into Another Project

Chapter 21   Getting into another project

Now that you have bought and flipped your property, your next step is to do it again. These are the steps of turning this into a business, with a lot of luck and a lot of flipped properties you will have the money to turn this project into a larger company. Your first project can turn a small profit but when spread over your entire investment could easily be a 20% return annually. It is important to make sure a piece of that profit is returned to the next project. The key is to start by doing most of the work yourself and slowly expand outward.

Let's go through some hypothec numbers just to give you a little perspective. If you invest $150,000 into a property for the total project and it takes you six month to turn the property and sell it. You see a 10% return on your money and you return 50% of your profit to the pile to make more money. Your $150,000 will become $165,000 from your first project. A return of $15,000 on your first property flipped. Now you returned $7,500 for the next your next project, so you now have $157,500 total cash to use. Your second property has a return of 10% as well and it sells for $173,250. On just this property you made $15,750 which is a 10% return but your increase in investment brought your total money earned on your properties for the year to $30,750. You will get to pocket $7,500 from the first project, $7,875 from the second project and put $15,375 into your investment pool. Your total you can spend on the next project is $165,375. This example was based on you being able to pocket some cash for your trouble but it would obviously be more helpful to your cause if you kept all your money in the pile, if possible. This would require another source of income and unless you have a lot of money it would probably come from a spouse's income to support you while you build this business. More than a 20% return is not uncommon on a year's worth of flipping. This is actually kind of low if you know what you are doing and some projects take losses even for experienced flippers.

If you could see a 20% return on your money each year you could double your initial investment in less than 5 years because of the fact you continue to reinvest back into your company. This sounds amazing but you also have to factor in, you no longer have the $150,000 to go on trips, buy cars or upgrade your own property. Also this will have become your primary occupation especially if you have no infrastructure built into your company. You will work all day, every day and have no free time because you are doing all the work on your projects yourself.

If you like the business you will want to get into a second property. The attractiveness of a lot of money and the thrill of the auctions can be addictive. Just remember to build a model of how you want to do each phase and stick to it. You will minimize your chances for failure that way. The rush of the first property will set in and you will see a future in the business of flipping. The second property will not feel like the huge headache it is going to be and you will jump in with both feet. If you do not feel that and the first project hurt your wallet more than it helped, stop now. The business is not for you, at least the first one did not take up too much of your time, go find another investment opportunity to put your money into.

Chapter 22

Becoming a Larger Company

Chapter 22   Becoming a larger company

Once you have some years of experience under your belt you will want to start expanding outward. It will take some time before you can bring in a modest amount of help. Your company will start expanding rapidly once you get to a point of having multiple millions to play with. The next thing you know you will be sitting in a corner office and a good chunk of your professional life will be over.

The stress of doing all the work yourself will eventually get to a point where you have to bring in some help. Most people start with drivers, they are relatively cheap to hire and they take a lot of the driving around off your hands. These are the people who drive to each property before the sales to check the condition of the property and report back to you. The next most common people hired are bidding agents they go to the sales and do the work of buying the properties for you, so you can stay in the office. You can also hire construction people at any point along the way. Whether they have been there since the beginning or not, as contracted workers, you will have to start bringing in your own people. People to do the work and people to oversee the work as you get to a point of not leaving your office. This is the base structure of expanding your business, you eventually have to get to the point of doing your work from your desk.

Eventually these will not be enough people to make your machine work. You will need to start your own real estate agency and hire your own agents, to buy and sell your properties. You will also need to start your own leasing agency, to deal with the rental properties you have put on your books and to bring in new business from outside your in house properties. You will need your own escrow company to take care of the escrows of your properties to help lower the costs of buying and selling each property. You will also need your own in house construction company. At this point your company is starting to look more like a large company.

You will be buying from the MLS, trustee sale and any other place you can find a discount on a piece of property. Your company will be to a point where it has to feed on all these pieces of land to feed the people it employs.

When you get to the point where you just make the executive decisions on the main matters of the company and overseeing the financials of the company your company has become a machine that nearly runs itself. You will be much older and have been in the business for many years. It is not a great idea to get the lofty idea that you will be sitting in the corner office of your building. This business is dangerous and many experienced companies go downhill from bad decisions, overly excited buyers and quick changes in the housing market. It is just a good idea to know how to get there in case things start going very well for your business. There is a lot more to do than the things I have listed but these are the general things that move your company along. To be at this point you would be buying in dozens of counties

and multiple states but you could potentially be a
multimillionaire.

Chapter 23

One Man Operation vs. Company Machine

Chapter 23   One man operation vs. company machine

You will find as you start out in this business the only person you will be able to rely on is yourself. After years of experience your operation will grow to incorporate more people and employees. It takes a proven track record in the business and a steady stream of income to support the company machine. This is a tough business and there will be many pit falls along the way but a driven successful business can become very prosperous.

When you start out in this business it will just be you doing the work. So let's give you an idea of what a day will look like. You will get up very early in the morning to check the lists of properties set to go to sale that day, at the trustee sales, in the area you feel comfortable buying in. You will go through the list eliminating anything that falls outside of your chosen buying criteria. Anything that has an opening bid at trustee sales you would comp and do title. Throwing out anything that you can not make money on and driving to all the rest of the properties on your list. You will then go to the trustee sales spending most of the business day there running comps and doing title from the sales site on the properties as they get bids. Bidding on the properties that you find you can make money on and possibly buying one or two. You will then drive to those properties you purchased assessing the property, its occupancy and your possible repair costs. Calling any contractor you need to give you prices on the things you can not accomplish on your own. Later going home very late at night to get the list prepped for the next day if you plan to buy more properties.

If you can only buy one at a time and/or you plan to do the work yourself on the property. You will spend the rest of your time dealing with the tenants in the property and making repairs on the property. Until it comes time to go buy something else this will keep you very busy. Remember time is very important on a flip and you need to get the property back on the market.

Evictions take time and so do repairs when you do them yourself. You will spend every minute of everyday dealing with the property to get it back on the market.

If you plan to do this as a hobby it is not a vital to go at break neck speed to get everything done. This will take a different model, expecting to rent out the property or buying low enough that the market changes will not affect your selling price negatively. I can tell you if you plan to do this as a hobby with a full time job. You will have no social or family life because your work will require you to spend all your free time on your project even to do the project slowly. I would not recommend attempting to do a property flip as a hobby. It increases your risk on each property exponentially.

As you build your business to incorporate people to help you, you will require more and more cash inflow to pay all the people you now employ. You will be covering peoples taxes and insurance as required by law when you have employees. You can also 1099 employees as subcontractors but there are legal requirements that you need to read through to understand if they can be considered subcontractors. Make sure to read up on both employees and subcontractors before bringing people into your operation, which will explain the advantages of both types.

As you become a large company you will feel the burden of doing all the work will slowly be released so that you can function like a normal person. This is not a quick change and will take many years before any type of change happens. The distinct advantage to the company becoming large is simply more gets done, more properties are acquired, more money is made and you have some free time. Running a large company is not a simple task, it will require many hours of your day also. You may not be doing all the work to do the flip on each property but you will be keeping up on the business of running the business. If a large company is not taken care of and protected by good employees it will fall apart as slowly as a sinking ship.

The only people or groups that can start their business out at the top of the food chain, with a large business, are the very wealthy and existing large companies. A million dollars will not cut it in this business, you need hundreds of millions in buying power to just become a large flipping company. This is why hedge funds and large investment groups jump into the business from time to time. The advantage you have by building the company up is the advantage of experience. Hedge funds use models and formulas to pick and flip their properties. They generally hire experienced flip companies to do their dirty work and the companies get paid a fee for the purchase of each property. This means those hedge funds are prone to large losses if their formulas are wrong. They must incorporate into their numbers a certain amount of loss over all of the purchases they make. This is assuming they will lose some money over their properties. It is smart in any business to assume some lose from some of the properties purchased but their numbers are much larger than an experienced buyer would be willing to tolerate.

Everyone hopes to someday become rich by starting a successful business. It is important to be realistic as you grow your company. You do not get to buy one property and be an expert in the business. You also do not get to buy a few properties and decide to become a giant company the next day. You will work and work until it almost grows on its own or you will push too hard and find yourself broke.

Chapter 24

Downfalls of the Business

Chapter 24   Downfalls of the business

As mentioned many times, this business is very dangerous and risky for your money. There are as many ways to lose money in this business as there are ways to make money. It is important to know some of the things to look out for to help minimize your possible risk. Each flip will carry its own set of risks and if you can see where things could go wrong you will be less likely to make those mistakes. If you do make those mistakes you will learn to not make them again.

When you are looking to buy a property you need to try to find and determine all possible downfalls before making the purchase whether it is at trustee sale or buying off the MLS. Minimizing the risk will allow you to offset what you plan to spend on the property and help make the decision if the property should be purchased at all. When buying a property from the MLS you will be looking for things like purchase price to market value ratio, repair costs to make the property marketable at your higher price, real estate agency fees and closing of escrow costs, possible issues with the title of the property and liens like back property taxes and current market trend costs such as property styles and increases or decreases in purchases prices in the area. There are many more things to list but these are the important things to look for. If they are missed or not appreciated for their individual risks you could easily lose money on your purchase.

When buying a property from trustee sales all of the previously mentioned risks are involved in your consideration of a property. Plus you also have to consider risks of buying from trustee sales which can include lack of ability to see inside the property, previous owners or renters abuse of the property, other types of liens which require payment, being at the right sales location and having your homework done for each property. Again there are more things that could be here on this list and things appear in any interaction with a property that are not always foreseen. Your preparedness will be the outstanding factor on whether you make money or not.

At low points in the market many people see properties as a get rich quick scheme. The market gets overly crowded with new player and larger corporations attempting to build fortunes in the real estate markets. If you try to become overly competitive with large companies, hedge funds and new comers to the business you will lose. Your safe bet is to do what you do, how you do it and let them destroy themselves by over spending on properties. If you reduce your profit margins too much you will run a huge risk of losing a large amount of money if you made a mistake. You need to have enough cash reserves in your business to be able to weather the storm until they leave. New comers and new large companies know less than you about the market and will make mistakes until profit margins fall or the small companies fold up and give up on the business.

Once you own the property it important to keep the building cost within your budget and save on costs where ever you can. Repairs can easily destroy your profits if you start making unnecessary changes. Thinking that your properties have a reputation of being great or poor quality can become a form of pride that will draw your business down. Even if you are known in the business no one knows why or how you do what you do or what areas of the business you make the most money. Do not let your ego get in the way of making the property make money.

When selling the property it is smart to have a real estate agent you trust to market your property properly. An agent who will not make efforts to find more ways to make more money off of you is what you need to look out for when looking for a sales agent because some agents will send you to vendors who give them kick backs for bringing them other services. This is not necessarily legal but they can find legal ways around the laws for such matters. These vendors can range from loan providers, escrow companies and anything related to getting services you need for your property provided by them. It is always best to be your own agent on your own property it is smarter for you and your money.

The biggest downfall of this business is the lawsuits. You will be involved in many lawsuits. Whether they are lawsuits you file or others have filed against you. Sometimes you are incidentally involved because you bought a property where the previous owner was overly sue happy. Whatever way you end up involved in a lawsuit you need to have good representation and having some basic legal knowledge is not a bad idea either. You should either have a good property lawyer on retainer or be able to find a good one quickly because in this business you will end up in court at some point and it will not be a onetime thing. You will need to be able to sue people too, you are given some sets of rights when you buy and sell these properties and you need to be ready to tell a previous owner they owe you money or protect what is owed to you in a real estate sale. Sometimes you get locked into escrow with someone for months and the buyer just can not get a loan approved. If you wrote it into the agreement the deposit will become yours. Buyers normally do not want you to have that money, because they want to try to use their deposit again and you generally have to sue in small claims court to get it. Sometimes people will sue you after the property is sold because things are not the way they want them in the house. You have to be able to protect your interests and the interests of your company. In real estate it is not a matter of if but when, so be aware of that.

What it comes down to is when people see you are trying to make money they will want to try to make money off of you. Always watch out for yourself, double check everything that is done for you and get people to work for you that you can trust to provide the services you need. If you do not you will get walked on, make mistakes and allow everyone else to make all the money while you pay to lose money and your valuable time on a project. Enough losses on enough properties will drive even the richest and strongest companies to the poor house.

Chapter 25

The Good Side of the Business

Chapter 25   The good side of the business

Now that you are scared by all the draw backs of the business you should know this business can be great for your wallet. It can be a very profitable venture if you stay ahead of the game. If you plan to get into the business and play your cards right you can make millions of dollars buying and selling real estate.

If you put your money into a bank you will make between .01%-6.0% annual interest on your money in a savings account depending on the current banking market factors and the economy. If you put your money in the stock market you could make, in a safe fund, 5%-25% annual interest. This is not saying you could not make much more in the stock market but you could also lose money in the market. I am using the idea you have your money in a safer stock, investment fund, commodity or bond. In the housing market you could easily make a 50% annual return on your money. If you buy and sell smart and do not get greedy there are points in the market where even a tight ship operation that is normally fairly low yield will return a large percentage.

The advantage to buying real estate is your money is backed by something, property. When you buy a property your money does not just disappear into the wind. You have something to show for where that money went. You do not own 1 ten thousandth of a percent of a company, like in the stock market. You own a piece of land, with a building on it, a hard tangible investment. If you are afraid you will lose money on it you can wait until the other end of the cycle and hold on to the property until you are certain you will make money. Property investment is a very smart and solid way to make money, if you play it smart.

Once people see you are starting to make money, investors, friends and family will all want to see what it is all about. Be careful who you let into your business because some people will want to steal your knowledge and do it for themselves. If you want people to become a part of what you are doing you will be happy to see your friends and family start making money along with you. As long as they understand the large risk they are taking by becoming a part of your business.

I have seen countless people in this business meet spouses from this business, become hugely wealthy, get lots of toys, extra properties for themselves, meet great friends and build large companies. You can become very successful from this business, sometimes all you need is a little luck and a lot of knowledge to do it. As long as you are smart with how you spend your money you could acquire the knowledge to do it too.